Also by Marc Kaminsky

Poetry

Kafka's Ax (2018)
Shadow Traffic (2008)
Target Populations (1991)
The Road from Hiroshima (1984)
Daily Bread (1982)
A Table with People (1982)
A New House (1974)
Birthday Poems (1972)

Prose

What's Inside You It Shines Out of You (1974)

Editor

Stories as Equipment for Living: Last Talks and Tales of Barbara Myerhoff. Co-edited with Mark Weiss in collaboration with Deena Metzger (2007)
Remembered Lives: The Work of Ritual, Storytelling and Growing Older, by Barbara Myerhoff (1992)
The Uses of Reminiscence (1984)
The Book of Autobiographies (1982)
The Journal Project: Pages from the Lives of Old People (1980)

Theater Pieces

In the Traffic of a Targeted City (1986)
Worksong (in collaboration with The Talking Band, 1978)

A CLEFT IN THE ROCK

poems

Marc Kaminsky

DOS MADRES
2018

DOS MADRES PRESS INC.
P.O.Box 294, Loveland, Ohio 45140
www.dosmadres.com   editor@dosmadres.com

Dos Madres is dedicated to the belief that the small press is essential to the vitality of contemporary literature as a carrier of the new voice, as well as the older, sometimes forgotten voices of the past. And in an ever more virtual world, to the creation of fine books pleasing to the eye and hand.

Dos Madres is named in honor of Vera Murphy and Libbie Hughes, the "Dos Madres" whose contributions have made this press possible.

Dos Madres Press, Inc. is an Ohio Not For Profit Corporation and a 501 (c) (3) qualified public charity. Contributions are tax deductible.

Executive Editor: Robert J. Murphy

Illustration & Book Design: Elizabeth H. Murphy
www.illusionstudios.net

Typeset in Adobe Garamond Pro & Bookman Old Style
ISBN 978-1-948017-03-9
Library of Congress Control Number: 2018932280
Cover Split Rock Photograph: Copyright © Jim & Penny Caldwell,
All Rights Reserved, Split Rock Research Foundation
www.splitrockresearch.org

First Edition
Copyright 2018 Marc Kaminsky
All rights reserved. No part of this book may be reproduced or transmitted in any form or by any means graphic, electronic or mechanical, including photocopying, recording, taping or by any information storage or retrieval system, without the permission in writing from the publisher.
Published by Dos Madres Press, Inc.

To Maddy, with love

TABLE OF CONTENTS

Prologue: On the Site of Loss

   Janus 3

I. A Narrow Room on Mt. Hope Place

   Days of Kivi 7
      1. I haven't seen you in six months
      2. When I come near you
      3. That stony face
      4. Head
      5. And you go on
      6. With your recitals in nursing homes
      7. Kivi you went crazy
      8. I stayed home from work
      9. Kivi you took me by storm
   Shiva for Kivi   19

II. My Own Private Diaspora

   Displaced Persons   23
   The Siege in the Room   27
   A Cleft in the Rock   30
   The Stranger's Table   39
   The Burning Hoop   41
   The Knot   43
   Stranded Objects   46
   The Word   48
   The Screen   49
   Refugees   53
   In Eldorado Springs   55

III. Sanctuary

    Collapsing Disbelief 63
    Instead of Confusion 64
    Benghazi 65
    Inside the Imaging Machine 66
    Awakening 68
    Encounter with a Swordsman 70
    Housework 73
    Metastasis 76
    Black Site 78
    The Eye of Your Pain 79
    In the Year of Chemotherapy 81
    In Sickness as in Health 82
    Outburst 83
    The Ordinary Life 85
    Love's Body 86
    Wisteria 89

IV. After a Brief Visit to Herring Point

    On This Shore 93
    At Herring Point 95
    Make Your Home Here 98
    Vows 100
    It's Not Too Late—If 101
    Before the Firmament 102
    Snow Geese 103
    The Return 105
    The Waves 110

Acknowledgments 113
About the Author 115

Prologue: On the Site of Loss

Janus

We never quite expelled you, god
of doors, gates and all beginnings
who faced in two directions at once

provisioner of paradox who
sustained the ins and outs
of more-than-human loves and days

you were demoted to an either/or
proposition, rebuked and scorned
as a hypocrite, kept on

as a trinket, stamped out
of lead, gold-plated and hung
on a bracelet, little deity

whose image, tamed
by reason, we retained
as decorative

we who are poor in
household gods and their
alchemy of everyday life

half recognize our need
for your charm, even
as we don't like to admit

that our desire for meta-
physical adventures
has turned us into collectors

of lost semantic potential
of which you are one
of the irrepressible placeholders.

I. A Narrow Room on Mt. Hope Place
In memory of my brother Akiva (1945-1986)

Yiddish is a motherland where one of us can understand the other one better—you hear? It's not only a *mama-loshn*, a mother tongue, but a motherland. Land we didn't have, we couldn't own, but Yiddish, and the things we carry with us in Yiddish—this no one could take from us. I would like you to be more involved with Yiddishkeit, and more in the Yiddish language too. You have it. I want you to continue living in it.
—Esther Schwartzman
(maternal grandmother of Marc, Akiva, and Riva)

For this I studied history?—the first in the family to graduate college—for this? To be a housewife and slavey straightening up the mess you leave behind? You get to go off to God-knows-where and I'm stuck here on Mt. Hope Place, living the same life my grandmother did in the shtetl.
—Mintzie Kaminsky
(mother of Marc, Akiva, and Riva)

> I embrace you as a brother.
> You cry like a son
>   —like a man who would like to be my son
> as I would like to be your father.

> *

> My brother's blood still cries out from the earth
> and calls me by my name.
>   —Peretz Kaminsky (father of Marc, Akiva, and Riva)
>   and author of "Cain," in *Adam, Cain and Other Prayers*

Days of Kivi

1

I haven't seen you in six months I try not to think of it Kivi
you turn up in my bad dreams last night I caught you screwing
    my wife
next thing I knew you threw an enormous blond forearm and
    thigh over my laid-out body
you rested on top of me, graceful sarcophagus effigy resting atop
    of his rotself
Dead weight of you crushed me
crushed the life out of me going to pommel the life out of you
Kivi I don't like the sound of this

Kivi my nightmare bedfellow Kivi friendliness of the flesh
it comes back to me contact of your skin and my skin Indian
    wrestling in the corridor funfights in the closet
And the summer night I watched over your sleep-loosened body
    in first manhood a decade ago
we used to take baths together Mama got anxious two little boys
    naked and splashing each other
the physical gladness comes back to me now I receive these
    memories with relief
in mourning

On my way home from work or Saturdays going down sidestreets
    I keep seeing people who turn out
not to be you
Kivi

2

When I come near you your face turns stony
I hold back my news rein myself in give up my animation scared
    to death of frightening you Kivi I'm sick
of being threatened by your sickness of being threatened by me

Kivi my most intimate friend Kivi the secret adversary spoiling
    my friendships
Kivi dweller in tents childhood life-raft partner fighting off sharks
    from a Kew Gardens Hills front porch
my easy companion fellow of a thousand anti-Mama campaigns
remember the caravans we robbed together the white sheets we
    propped up with a broomstick in bed our oasis our Sahara
    hideaway Sunday mornings till Papa got up

In the days when we played together we invented sandstorms
    and giant waves with teeth in them
Mama raged early and late against the waste of her life, a
    housewife and slavey condemned to straightening up after us
Papa was off in a corner writing his Cain poems, confessing
    his wish to murder his brother and win the Nobel Prize
Bubba crammed our homeland—the Yiddish language—into our
    narrow apartment we drifted through deserts and oceans
    where no one could find us isolated together
I was dumb as a fish in its fishy element I couldn't feel you
    shivering on the other side of the room
when Mama came down on you hard I wanted to protect you

If you say this is bullshit I'll tell you not to forget
we lay head-to-head in the one bedroom 15 years we looked out
    onto Mt. Hope Place from the same window three stories up
we closed the door against the same intruders midnights we
    whispered a little

Who else but you
was with me when I lay under the eerie regime of cold brightness
    climbing the sky
rising over the roofs of East 176th Street mooning over us pale
    head with no eyes briefly crowned with TV antennas
then up to the vast place over everything an airy refuge in which
    we and the sadness of the Bronx floated
filling the room with light
Kivi your flashes of trust mean the world to me

3

That stony face
the face of December 1968 is staring down at me

when you were Yahweh omnipotent in wrath and by turns the
    wronged brother Esau heading north

I keep trying to follow you to appeal to you to prove I am not
    the one
you imagine I imagine the miracle of the early days of 1969
    when we were together

your fixed stare lost its spike lips parted amiable flesh tones shine
    of merciful blood-warmth we spoke without hindrance

but always the flush ices over the mask that declares the death
    sentence comes back

4

Head
    up there in parts unknown with the balls of the eyes about to
explode the musculature of the cheeks rigid
but ticking
everything in you stopped and speeded up at the same time
you look down on me from your high place
with pity for the ex-hero of your childhood whom you are about
    to depose

with your trips to the mental Indies with Huichol sacraments
    disguised as brownies with discount bananas in your sour
    cream
with Mama in the aisles of the A&P of your brain bargain-hunting
    for day-old bread
palpating cantaloupes at passing fruit stands meditating on
    Donne's "Anniversaries"
with coconuts eating the white meat inside citing the broken
    shells as bits of Kabbalah
letting them pile up on the table lifting them high in the air
    chanting mysteries
stroking their kinky textures mixing everyone up with allusions
    to God-knows-what laced with hints of sagas cruising Times
    Square
with clenched fists you tell of all-night meets at Bickford's taking
    on all comers
with one-upping the Shakespeare scholar at the West End Bar
    the novelist at Rienzi's stealing the medical student's date at
    Carnegie Hall
doing lines of coke at the Port Authority Bus Terminal
with the Louisiana runaway you picked up at Grand Central
    Station kept a few days and turned over to your buddy Carl

with City College girls from Riverdale drawing lots using cruel
    methods
you end each episode in silent fury or a short burst of laughter
    throwing down the challenge—Can you beat this?

with your universal erudition making you fit to take on Professor
    H. who gave you a C on your *Troilus* paper
with dropping out of the CUNY doctoral program to concentrate
    on your opera career

5

And you go on

with your knowing way of nosing in-between couples
with Marlovian lines splendidly scaring off small fry
and your mindblowing metaphysics offered up hour after hour
    to Bubba at the Pesakh seder

with your feats of linguistic analysis
with your harmonium practicing Schubert lieder
with your closets full of Japanese prints you sold through the
    mail three years making a living

I drove you to Malden, Massachusetts with a U-Haul carting
    your Japan packets 200 miles
small-town Catholics beat you up in the street bearded Jew
    hippie addressing 12-year-old girls a moral pestilence
with a U-Haul I drove you back to the Bronx to three paralyzed
    months on Mama's sofa

You began to be not obese but imposing
with your capes and swagger and forensic conquests you became

    Akiva Kaminsky performing being himself in the grand manner
on the Hudson Valley Line passengers whispered as you passed
word got out that you were an Italian count and graciously
you acknowledged the astonishment you stirred up and down
    the aisles with a nod of the head

6

With your recitals in nursing homes interrupted by occasional
    thuds canes slipping out of palsied fingers
rows and rows of white-haired or blue-tinted or bald heads
    nodding in time beaming up at you adoring your full young
    basso
with Papa in the peach-colored auditorium eating you up
with Bubba taking credit after the concert
with your voice still filling the room with memories of voices
    still in bloom

with the tenderness in you coming out finding a haven among
    the old ones

with singing Leporello's arias on subway stations zapping the
    rush hour
with a courteous word to a cursing salesman zapping the
    bourgeois mentality
with your zap gun ready for use at Cousin Harriet's wedding
with frantic subway excursions to the Bronx to conduct hearings
    in the case of Papa
with acts of inquest with orphanage silences
with your breakfasts on Sunday mornings at Bubba's an open
    secret driving Mama to fits of jealous shrinktalk
with egging on Riva to make it with your pals

with your 10-by-10 cubicle in an SRO brownstone off Central
    Park West your home since the Malden fiasco
with hardly enough room to get to your dining room table the
    piano stool
with gates on your windows grand ballroom ceilings 18-feet-high
    bookcases towering on either side of the upright piano like
    the façade of a Gothic cathedral in miniature
with late-night TV days you speak to no one but your mirror
with your spanking new dungarees topped by a starched white
    shirt with black bow tie
antique gold watch chain draped over your stomach a graduation
    gift from the folks
with your Einstein hair

with your nonstop performances in all five boroughs repeating
    the old repertoire at senior centers and homes for the aged
with your commanding come-on you reduced the Palestinian girl
    to three small mounds of quietness and excitement you said
you have hearty tête-a-têtes with her mother who loves to feed you
with your letters to famous men of letters winning respectful
    responses to your theoretic
with Marshall McLuhan and Theodor Reik encouraging you to
    continue your investigations
with your pot in a cheese box on your window sill
with the mystical poetry you write to plow up asphalt and tarmac
    and release lost spirits reenchanting the world
with your Mafia supplier meeting you at the Hadassah bazaar
with dealing ounces cut-rate to the cognoscenti at small-press
    book fairs and to your regulars on the corner of Columbus
    and 83rd
with your appreciative laugh coming a bit too soon

with making the rounds at all hours getting thrown out
of Mama's house for acting weird making insulting remarks just

before the dinner guests were due to arrive dignitaries from
    the world of Jewish communal service
trying Bubba's next looking to score a salvific connection nothing
    doing
from there back up Gun Hill Road under the Woodlawn-Jerome
    tracks past the cemetery
to Riva and Norman's near the reservoir crazy with cold
    shoes soaked through by the snow
freaking them out in no time
and so turning up at my place a day later in the slush dead of winter
an old Russian army greatcoat thrown over your shoulders one
    of the hand-me-downs you got from me worn like a mantle
empty sleeves dangling fists pounding against my door, crying
Brother! brother! brother! brother! open up!

7

Kivi you went crazy believing my hex was the real power blocking
    your genius career
you cracked up in December 1968 you unraveled me
marching through my doorway like General de Gaulle under the
    Arch of Triumph
passing through my rooms as if they were old Nazi headquarters
looking into cabinets and closets for evidence sniffing into Rita's
    underwear drawer

when you got the shakes and tore the royal red comforter from
    our bed and wrapped it around you
your face frozen and glaring
ordering tea demanding I serve you
speaking incomprehensible sophistries in a Richard Tucker
    profundo
between conundrums telling me what a shmuck I am how you
    pitied me

what a fool you'd been for submitting to the old law of
    primogeniture blinded to your own
stature you the all-round man and match of anyone you might
    meet in the night of your wanderings
grand unmasker of lies emigrant who made the crossing out of
    family exile into ploughshare Zion
with hatred radiating out of your monumentality a shape
    disembodied by robes
immobile ghastly
you said I ripped off your brain waves you had come back for them

when you stripped and wriggled nakedly around the kitchen
    flapping your hands singing a little falsetto reprise la-di-day
then folded your legs under you suddenly like a camel and sat at
    my feet looking up with mocking disciple eyes
which turned to blue ice declaring tyrannicide
with the knife gleaming on the counter a pulse away from your
    right hand
afraid for my life I saw you at last I saw
                                         you cast off
the delusive and wretched sanity
                                     that denied you your birthright
and assert the truth of every child born
                                           that the last shall come first

8

I stayed home from work for a week I was in mourning
Rita held me all night I wept I spewed out the stories every night
    for a week she stayed up with me
stories
        of how I got the paint sets and the praise all my guilt
at having been favored

What's so unusual about that? Rita said

I told her how Papa favored my gifts over yours in exchange for
    the paintings I made
he raised me up in the house as the son in whom his greatness
    was plainly visible

An old story, Rita said

Crushed by your memories I cried how you ran after me at age
    four calling my name in Yiddish
I left you behind to play with my friends the six-year-olds who
    didn't call me Moti

What do you imagine you did that was so terrible? Rita said

and once age eight I went wild with rage Mama and Papa couldn't
    pin me down to their bed
with my arms breaking loose my legs flailing dangerously my
    voice hoarse with screaming
I want to kill Kivi! I want to kill him!

How human! how human! Rita said

I told her that when you were born they snuck you into the
    house while I was sleeping they hid you in their bedroom
thanks to Bubba's offer of help the opening move in her
    campaign to move back into the Old World three-generation
    household and spend her days working alongside her daughter
she shamed Mama for giving way to her lust blamed her for
    getting pregnant and going through with the unplanned
    pregnancy
depriving her little baby boy her Moti her first-born her
    moshiakhl of the total attention he needed

so Mama handed you over to Bubba who fed and bathed and
    changed you in secret for two years they divided us between
    them
in the name of protecting me from the jealousy that led Mama
    and Papa to cut their brothers out of their lives
through the actions they took to spare us this fate they transmitted
    it to us
two brothers living inside our parents' story that made room for
    only one to thrive
you were the dirty secret in their bedroom I wasn't allowed to see
    Mama caring for you
I have no memory of the day they opened that door and you
    crawled out

How come you never told me this before? Rita said

It wasn't there to be told I don't know it seemed to have never
    happened or happened in a dream in another country
a dream I forgot we lived in hiding I didn't know what was going
    on in that room until Kivi brought it home to me

9

Kivi you took me by storm you destroyed my obliviousness you
    forced me to face the damage I'd done
unknown to myself you were unknown to me when we were
    four-armed and fighting the same sea or huddled under the
    one tent
in that narrow room we lay head-to-head every night of our
    childhood meeting in dreams the self-
same myth that made a scapegoat-messiah out of the first-born
    son and a scapegrace-rival out of the second one
I believed my place was to shine always to shine and to hell with
    everything else

After you walked out of my living room on that day of reckoning
    I called home
I said, Kivi's in trouble you've got to help him find help for him
    talk to him he needs you I need you to come over now we
    have to talk
Papa put aside his indignation bewilderment shame at your
    behavior in front of the dinner guests he came immediately
I told him you thought I was the cause of your craziness
He answered in his sardonic omniscient voice, Well, aren't you?
Words I didn't know I had in me sprang to my lips I was surprised
    as he was when I heard myself
say, No, I wasn't his parents!
He turned white his mouth fell open uttering, Oh my God!

And the spell under which I'd labored was broken
and Kivi was broken and I was
broken

it took all this murderousness and madness
for you and me to break
out of the family lie

Now you and I will have to find out who
we are each one in his own
separate diaspora

Written in March, 1969
Revised in 1970, 1976, 1984, 1987,
1990, 2011, 2013, 2016

Shiva for Kivi

I wrote those lines nearly 20 years ago unable to finish the poem
    I never intended to abandon you were 23 I was 25 in those days
Sunday 3 a.m. the phone rings a voice says it's Akiva your brother
    he's dead he died suddenly a heart attack an hour ago
I called Riva we waited until dawn then went up to the Bronx to
    tell them

Our mother seeing two of her children leaning before full daybreak
    in the doorway shrieked what's wrong
we told her Kivi died he had a heart attack and he died she fell
    to the floor
and he fell with her an old man and frail now he let go of his cane
    and let himself down with care
then raised his arm and brought down his fist against the rug three
    times a gesture that seemed unreal in its moment
but later repeating it in the imagination I saw it was a ritual
    movement an act of will to bring on the uncontrollable grief
    that he needed more time to feel his mind being quicker to
    take in the news than his heart to believe it could be
that Kivi was dead

We buried you Kivi age 41 the day before Passover we came home
    to no seder
and sat down at a *tish mit mentshn* a table with people although
    it's forbidden to sit shiva during the holiday
we told stories of Kivi

You came to my house last Thanksgiving our era of silence ended
you walked over to where I was working picked up a knife
    wordlessly we chopped broccoli together a while

and our mother happening by just then stopped in the door-
    way to listen to witness
a moment that fed her hope that she'd live to see her children
    gather around her and restore her
shattered family

                                April 18, 1986

II. My Own Private Diaspora

Displaced Persons

1

Every night I fell asleep traveling
in my father's song
to the east, to the west.

In the east he taught me
death, in the west
he taught me death.

He sang of going under in the black
fires of Warsaw
and the crematoria.

He sang of being wrapped in white
linen in the streets of Laredo
and St. James' Infirmary.

For much of my life I wasn't here,
hypnotized by my father's
ghastly lullabies.

I traveled on in images and music
he made more real to me
than my own right hand.

2

Frightened by the dreams
my father left me
with, I fought

sleep in that narrow
bed. I imagined myself
awake in my coffin.

My father's eyes
peered over the edge,
crying at last. Next

thing I knew I was
jammed onto a train
to oblivion.

The trip went on night
after night. I'm still traveling
there.

3

By day the children
of survivors I
work with tell me

their dreams, at night
I join them on
the unloading ramp.

Sticks, clubs, curses.
There I wait, amid
piles of suitcases. Later,

emptying and sorting them,
I see my father's *Tehillim*
and bottle-lens reading glasses.

4

Amid my father's captivating
lamentations, I was most
himself, the one

displaced into the one
who listens. Over time,
I trained my absence

to become a ware-
house of the past
where others

with a kindred malaise
could wander around
to claim a self

among the heaps
of baggage abandoned
by parents who lost

sight of them.
Of us. We don't
remember when and how

we were condemned to live
with something that obstructs
our movement, something

we collide against in hallways,
streets, bedrooms, we
are desperate to throw

our arms around it
and drag it
to the mirror where hunger

to own its existence
could conceivably force it
back into attachment

with its personal shape, yet
it goes on eluding
our grasp. A black cloth

covers each mirror in our house,
and every time our hands
reach out to pull it down,

we shrink back in confusion,
lest we meet our own
permanent loss of face.

The Siege in the Room

Without neck
muscles, your once leonine head
rolled away from your heaving
chest. We sat
at the foot of your bed,

watching over you. You
kept throwing off the sheet,
lifting your gown, tearing
the blue diaper off.
My sister whispered: Noah.

She is, like you, an exegete
of situations, removing the shock
of the never-met-before
by naming and living it as
a variation of Scripture.

My mother, after a twelve-hour
shift, after years of the unmaking
of the man who could no longer be
her life's companion, didn't want you
tearing strips of flesh

off the chickenbreast. She told you
to use your knife and fork.
You snapped your teeth at her
like a badger backed into a hole
by a larger animal. And I

drifted away from them, out
of the plate glass picture window
past a long wall in plunging
perspective that blocked most
of the view, until I reached

an expanse where the golden spire
of the Chrysler Building pierced
spongiform clouds, beyond them were
skies where you'd been afoot
with your vision, arguing with God

and visiting the cemetery in air
of those whose namelessness
you called "Jewsmoke
of the crematoria" in one of your poems
against shrouding our hearts from the horror.

I left the room when you fell
into a light sleep, I paced
up and down the corridor,
every wandering thought brought me
back to you: your teeth

in a glass jar on the windowsill,
your face deformed by their absence—
you were, even now, not less
to me than you yourself, the cries
wrung out of you by a nightmare

told me you were still at work
dreaming the Jewish centuries.
Legs racing in place, you cycled
between sleeping and waking,
writhing in cuffs that bound you

to the bars of the hospital bed,
you struggled to escape our care.
None of us could accompany you.
We went on making the human kind
of sense that shrinks in the presence of death,

we each held on to our own
conception of you, trying to keep you
alive as the person we'd known,
while you kept trying to make us feel
the horror of your continued existence.

A Cleft in the Rock

1

You died in the midst
of the portion of the week
where Moses pleads:
Let me behold Your presence.

You couldn't hold on
to this passage where
God answers: No man
may see My face and live.

You, father, believed
you were singularly rejected.
Even to Moses God says: See!
There is a place near Me.
Place yourself on that rock.

I will place you in a cleft
of the rock and cover you
with My hand while I pass by
and I will take away My hand
and you will see My back.

During all the bitter years
that you spent losing
your memory, you wanted to die.

At night you went to the study
where God's face had been
hidden from you.

You got down on your hands
and knees and crawled around
the room, pulling every plug
out of every socket.

2

After a lifetime of trying to slip out
of your grasp, I wanted to hold onto your presence
when it was ruthless to do so. I wanted more

time to caress your skull and shoulders
and see your clenched face open in wonder
as I told you the story of your life,

naming the titles of your books and grand-
children and describing the good deeds
you were amazed to learn were yours. But

you were too busy putting your last display
of ferocity to work, spitting your dinner
at nurses who wiped your spittle and gorge

off their faces and resumed their task
of bending you to their will so effectively,
you cried, Mama! I left the room

so I wouldn't have to see you put
on an IV drip with your hands tied
to the bars of the hospital bed,

while you writhed to slip through
the cleft in the rock over which
God turned His back on you.

3

At the shiva, I take comfort
in speaking of your anguish—
in this it's possible to live
in the illusion of your presence.

After everyone's gone, I sit
at your kitchen table, remembering:
it's as if you've just gone
off to your study to be with God,

who gave you the silent treatment
and returned you to the same eternity
you'd known since the time you dropped
unwanted into your mother's house,

deadlocked in a struggle that lasted
as long as you did. You clung
to your withdrawn God for
the nothing you got out of Him.

And I cling to you in my reverie,
taking my cue from your taste
for Jewish mysticism, I'm tempted
to cover the nakedness of your protest

in words of the Kabbalah where it can be
seen as a reverse act of faith.
In this latest absence, have you broken through
to God's hidden essence, the Eyn Sof,

the mystical cleft in the rock, the Nothing
in which you and the Eternal One meet
and the animus which was your magnificent cause
for being ceases? Or do you go on

demanding more from God than He can rain
upon you without putting out the black
fire of your works and days, which I hear
crying, Lord, here I am!

4

While here, you staggered
between the grandiose
and the prophetic, between
withdrawal and poetry.

I hated seeing
the self-display under which
you hid the harsh self-
knowledge you cut into

the rock of your poems
with the same hammering
rage and fine right
hand that guided the chisel

before you renounced
carving flow into stone.
Your will—the artist's will—
to make mute material speak

of an end to the war
between flesh and air
turned your every
work into the wrestling

that leads to surrender—
a form of prayer that I also heard
in your improvisations
at the piano after

the phrases in which
you'd stored your memories
were gone. Today I wake up
in the tremendousness

of your absence, feeling
that I don't feel it
acutely enough, I lie down
in the room where I've always been

closest to you—the night studio
where you burned through the misery
that froze your talent for naming
and scaling God's distance from you,

and I was warmed by the fire
that consumed your deadness when
writing became psalm and you pleaded with God
to let you hear His kindness at dawn.

5

In your solitude you wrote "a song
of adoration" that was added by the rabbis
to the *Siddur Lev Shalom*, the liturgy
for Sabbath and the Festivals. Too late

for you to cross back over the history
that separated you from your pious
grandfathers, who departed this world
scratching unreadable letters on the walls

of gas chambers, you couldn't
bring yourself to pray in the midst of
a living congregation of Jews, yet they
now recite your prayer on holy days:

> I stand revealed
> by all the songs I pray.
> My songs implore,
> insist
> that they be heard by You
> who dwell in all the distances
> outside of time and space,
> and yet,
> within all things.
>
> My songs and I,
> my prayers and contemplations,
> dream of penetrating
> to the secrets of Your name.
> I search your nomenclature
> for my identity
> and seek my features

in the image that You made.
I am choiceless in this quest,
except I sing of sorrow,
praise, and exaltation.

You are before all things,
and after them.
You bracket me within the horns
of void and nothingness.
You enfold me in the wings
of Your creation,
and then return me,
with the songs I pray,
to dust.

6

By dying, you got out
of the way of your poems.
The noise of your thundering
need, as you read them aloud,

kept the sheer words hidden,
drowned out their dryness.
The disdain you inspired in us,
your children, has nothing

to feed on now. What remains
is our love, and tears
of late recognition. We see
your work stripped

of the hunger you brought
us, while you gesticulated
toward the mountain
where you wanted us

to behold you declaiming.
You have gone through
the null place
where you fled to take

cover from the living.
Now in the rock, you
are growing splendid
in the character

you couldn't believe
you possessed while
you lived pythonlike
in our midst: you

wrapped yourself
around us and
crushed us to extract
the air you needed

to breathe in from us, lungs
out of which you craved hosannas.
We went dead rather than serve
as parts of your immortal body.

Now your voice ascends
from the desert
that was given to you
as the task of your life:

a trackless waste in which to remain
faithful to the Promise, while every step
brought you closer to the truth:
that the Lord sat you in darkness,

like those who were long dead,
and you would never set foot
in the place where God
dwells among living people.

The Stranger's Table

Four years at Columbia couldn't undo
the peddler's pack my folks tied
with the golden chain of Jewish
tradition onto vestigial wings I didn't know
I carried, I just felt weighted down
by dread—if I dared to ascend
in the world of the goyim I'd be dead.

So I trudged on, clinging to the way
my grandparents' fear of the world marked me
every time I entered a restaurant, I was afraid
that if I sat in the wrong seat, something
would attack from behind,
my line of escape would be closed
by Americans cracking lobster shells between
their molars and laughing, sucking the sweet meat
forbidden to me, as they casually held down the barriers
to my safety with their whole bodies.

I was taught to walk in another century
by Besarabian Jews in whose restless legs
under the table the readiness for flight
of our ancestors was passed down
from their generation to my own, my nervous
system could read any room as a trap
waiting to be sprung, a scene where unlawful
desires I didn't yet know were mine
hunted me like the hidden malice that could return
me to the ghetto at any moment.

What good would my Ivy League passport do
if my face was stamped *Jude*? My degree
in English gave me no exit
visa from my mother
country, Yiddish, the floating Pale
of anxiety was my first language. I needed plastic
surgery of the spirit, the kind Freud invented,
to remove the *pekl* that kept me stooped
and to help me grow, given my lack of
angel's wings, shoulder blades
minus their Lamarckian burden of having to fly
to another country where I wouldn't be
forced to make my way among hostile neighbors.

Note: *Pekl* in Yiddish means knapsack, package, bundle;
burden, bag of troubles.

The Burning Hoop

My brain stem never left the savannah.
What grace and misery it places
before my eyes, and the present

films over like a memory
of the present. Women go by me,
women on bare legs

the bareness of them grabs
my attention and hurls it across
the street toward another body

a bare neck, bare skin exposed
to the predator I find, against
everything I hold sacred,

is myself. Or not myself,
for I am hardly the body I was
a grace and misery ago.

•

In the hazard of these summer streets,
under the tracks of the elevated
subway stop, and also at the newsstand,

waiting for the light to change, anywhere
I congregate with the traces of all
the others I've been in my ascent

to this instant, among herds and djembes,
with the bristling of the hair on my neck,
walking on two feet, I am always telling

the sudden lion whose nearly invisible
rolling of his great shoulders and arching
closer to the ground signals the start

of his stalk, to stop it, and jump else-
where, through the burning hoop
I hold up, and come out of it

on the other side as a man, a walking
man, minus the mane of lust
I want to set flying in the wind.

The Knot

Who's Stevie Opert? I suddenly find myself wondering. The name comes back, but not the image of the person it refers to. At 66 going on 67, who can depend on his memory? But this is a reversal of the trick that memory usually plays on me. The name minus its object of reference—this is a first. I remember standing in front of our garden apartment in Kew Gardens Hills, something wonderful has happened, it's the first time I've ordered something and it's arrived in the mail, I'm in possession of the thing I most want—the Captain Video ring I saw advertised on our brand-new 7-inch TV is on my finger. And when I put its protuberant part in my mouth and blow, it lets out a high-pitched wailing whistle. In the Elijah stories my father tells me, Elijah the Prophet turns up to rescue people in need, just like Captain Video, only he's invisible and everywhere at once, on the sidewalk with me and standing beside a bare cupboard in a hovel on the other side of the ocean where he says to a poor couple he will grant them whatever they wish. In one voice they say they want food to fill their bellies, Elijah whistles and a feast is spread out before them, it's the miracle of Passover, my father tells me. Captain Video, I say, can hear this whistle wherever he is. Someone else is there, looking down at me, but every last physical trace of him has disappeared, in place of living memory is the gravesite of mythical safety on which I read the name of the absent figure. It's Stevie Opert. But now the oblivion parts, a hand reaches out of it, and Stevie Opert says he has a better trick to show me. With that, he kneels, pulls one of the ends of his shoelace and—presto!—it comes untied, then with the fingers of both hands moving faster than the eye can see, he restores the missing knot and stands up in triumph. I'm crushed. He has just tied his shoelace! He has just tied his so-called shoelace, even though he's wearing sneakers. But there's no escaping it, no word-magic can undo his feat. I understand what he has shown me: I'm a handful of dust, a puny thing dependent on the word of grown-ups, on the promise of being rescued, the miracle that children and people in misfortune believe in. But Stevie Opert has no need of such things, he has attained mastery over the knot that makes him self-sufficient, a boy-man secure in his shoes, ready to decide between fight or flight. I try to reassure myself with a quick calculation. I'm only six, I say. That leaves me four years until I'm old as you. Stevie Opert at ten also knots his tie, he walks above me, my upstairs neighbor. Looking back, I see a boy-child on a brand-new American street talking to someone who has already taken off and is out of earshot. That boy-child can't know how anxious I am for him, or that the anxiety that visits him now will cloud the rest of his childhood and afflict his youth, or that I will hear him, sixty years later, as I take my afternoon walk through city streets which are my theater of memory. Here I stumble upon him thinking, I'm only six, that leaves me only four years to get the skill that Stevie Opert has into my fingers. Already I feel the deadline rapidly approaching.

Stranded Objects

for Eric Santner

I'm 67, and I still don't know
what dust is, and why—when
you let things stand, things like
the ceramic duck tucked away
on the top shelf of my book-
case, something I never think
about unless I have to climb
up there to retrieve a back issue
of *New Left Review*—the duck
a gift from a lost
friend who had no idea what
to give me for my 50th—
countless mementos like that
stranded throughout my floor-
to-ceiling shelves on three
sides of the room where I am
most myself, losing and recovering
my train of thought—impossible
to hold all those things in mind, or
know why they acquire a
veil of it—dust, I mean dust—
that you can't see but under
which they tend toward a common
grayness—unless I come up
close to one of my stranded
objects, and see a layer of fine
particulate matter under which
it's faded, and carefully
run my index finger across
its surface to restore its color-
fulness into contact
with the air, out of which

the generation of dust goes on
grain by invisible grain gently
dressing the things I've collected
over a lifetime in a coat of oblivion.

The Word

for Mark Weiss

Delights in the word.
As in his neighborhood
pharmacy, with the pretty Dominican
cashier who's always been tight-lipped
above her plunging neckline

while ringing up his things
and handing him his change,
maybe taking his friendly interest
in her as an attempt to wring
a smile out of her face. Not

that he's insensible
of the roundness on each side
of the intriguing slope
of cleavage and all of it
tightly wrapped under an orange

sweater. Today she's sucking
delicately on a section
of something that reaches back
across decades and surprises
him with the word

he hasn't heard or read
in 50 years. Naranja? he asks her.
Is it called a naranja? Yes,
she smiles, and a long-averted
conversation begins at last.

The Screen

to Kate Farrell

At the window, racing
in place

I look through
innumerable tiny black squares

table and garden and chairs
covered in snow-drifts

breath taken
away as I pedal nowhere

•

My backyard under the wind-blown snow
changes into a world of rolling hills

and valleys, I'm stationed here
for the next half-hour on my exercise bike

•

Dark specks drop
from the sky, these are sparrows

come to peck
at the withered grass

under the quietness spread across
the little pocket of nature

I observe, I think of providence
in Hebrew the literal meaning

of *hashgahah peratis* is
detailed attention

•

Sparrows fall
on the other side

of the screen I
watch them rise

from the snow
and lose

sight of them
until they glide back

down, teasing sustenance
from the ground

•

In summer the wire mesh
let the wind blow through my hair

now in winter I ride
looking out of a closed window

and feel a rush
in the air

•

The sparrows dive
and fly, and I am a speck

of light streaming into this yard
part of a big mind

that follows these comings and goings
without a screen

although my attention is focused
through a practice or grid or cartoon

such as the old masters used
to transfer and enlarge a holy scene

•

Belief comes and goes
the sparrows in my mind

begin as an after-
image of a Biblical passage

not one sparrow shall fall
on the ground outside

the eye of Providence
there is nothing covered

that shall not be revealed
part of the stock of phrases

I walk around with, phrases
that spin in my head

like chip-chip chatter
until the moment I see them—

the sparrows
fluttering down

to the hard ground
in my yard, digging

up a root with powerful beaks, fiercely
jerking their heads

from side to side
determined to pull it out

pausing
in their labor

they let loose a clattering call
for all to hear

as if a screen unrolled
before my eyes

during my heart exercise
at my window

I picture them
just as they are

in an enclosed garden concealed
in a vast shroud of passing appearances

Refugees

Whoever got in my way
eviled me and—wham!
the hammer I acquired
from my father's tool-
chest of impatience
came down and cracked
my enemy's brains loose
when I was seven and lord
of the demesne where
my diaspora folks poured
ancestral nightmares
down the gullet of the day.

Now I'm stuck in another
country, wedged in
among tens of thousands
of cars belching toxic
fumes before the toll
plaza onto Goethals
Bridge, we roll
down our windows to
ask what happened.

One stalled mini-van
up ahead has brought
traffic to a halt
for miles and they
talk about evacuating
this area when a real
catastrophe comes
the meltdown of drivers
with nowhere

to go causes hands
to slam down on
horns blasting out-
rage six-ton behemoths
lurch forward fenders
miss each other by
inches engines revving
in idle brakes
scream we can't do
anything but hope no
one crashes into us.

The dystopian traffic
jam Godard depicted
forty years ago in *Weekend*
has become our Sunday
night fare, traveling back
to the city we sought to escape
from at the Jersey shore
we've traveled three
or four feet in the last
hour, but it dawns
on me I've remained
calm all this time.

The horizon between
this place of road rage
and my childhood frustration
opens now onto this
small refuge, thanks
to a life spent loving
you, I'm content
just sitting beside you,
friend and dear friend, two
in a deep-founded sheltering.

In Eldorado Springs

to Maddy

> He opened a rock and water flowed;
> in the desert rivers ran.
> —Psalm 105

1

Walking along a trail
at the edge of a precipice,
you turned as each new
wonder came into view

to show me your face
bursting into soundless
laughter, your eyes
communicated intensities

of delight and awe
that spoke to my whole
body like drum language
and placed me in the scale

of things never seen before.
With each step, I entered
the area of your surprise—
a vein of wilderness

through which shy rattlesnakes
slip in and out of the sun
and we become unobtrusive
so as not to disturb

the solitude of the mountain
lion and the green pastures
where elk come out
in the open to rut.

2

Below us the rushing
of Boulder Creek
broke into strings of white
water, thunder and mist

rose out of the waterfalls.
Down there we passed a sign
warning visitors not to
be fooled by the shallowness

of the stream, "its swiftness
quickly incapacitates you;
waders are rarely given
a second chance." Above us

tiny figures unsupported
by ropes and gear
climbed beyond what was formerly thought
possible, feeling their way

up the rock face, pressing
their bodies into the Front Range cliffs,
surveying the surface
with attentive fingertips

on the lookout for the next hand-
hold. I could just barely stand
watching their nearly motionless ascent.
They grasped the chance offered by

providence in the palm of one hand
and searched for survival with the other—
vertical pilgrims, seeking to elevate
each moment lived by risking death.

3

The Zuni and Arapaho brought
gods, rock face and mortals
together when they assembled here
to chant loudly and in unison,
"You have come out
standing at your sacred place."

4

Layers of rocks of many colors

skeins of geological time
unwind before my eyes

their porous skins marked by white
striations, long lines quivering in sand-
stone like squiggles recording a heart-
beat or a voice singing, wave after
wave follows the currents of vanished seas

uplifted out of the deeps
under which they were formed, they were forced
to jut at precarious angles against gravity
I stand at the edge
of a precipice, wonder and awe at the rock face
overcome my fear of heights.

5

Rock taking its face
from water, the below taking
its place with the above,

weight and erosion mixing
sand, water and time
into gigantic formations,

these ancient things
are the event
going on under our feet
as we walk here,

the divided plates
of the continent
move inchmeal over millennia
into unending collision,

pushing up into our day
what's at the bottom,
what's mute, what's
in the beginning.

6

Walking in the Rockies,
you gave me the amazement
of your first response,

and I lived the moment twice
over, seeing your pleasure,
then seeing the source of it,

I was taken beyond
your face and my happiness
in your happiness, and I

stood alone before the rock face,
keeping my balance, free
of my fear of death.

And now a third time
in the mountains, seeing
the two moments come together as

one memory, I am with you and with
the timelessness of the lost ocean
rushing through rock.

III. Sanctuary

The word metastasis, used to describe the migration of cancer from one site to another, is a curious mix of *meta* and *stasis*—"beyond stillness" in Latin—an unmoored, partially unstable state that captures the peculiar instability of modernity.... Cancer is an expansionist disease; it invades through tissues, sets up colonies in hostile landscapes, seeks "sanctuary" in one organ before immigrating to another.
 —Siddhartha Mukherjee, *The Emperor of All Maladies*

Collapsing Disbelief

I have no use for this
adversity. The enlightened attitude
of accepting the illness—
what violence against the integrity
of my love. The preliminary
diagnosis of lymphoma is kaput.
Your surgeon's voice on our
answering machine informs us
you have metastatic breast cancer.

No patience now for all
the little irritants I normally
tolerate well. But I know:
this is only a symptom
of my anger at God, the God
I don't believe in under
ordinary circumstances
has irrationally failed to
exempt you from this plague.

Instead of Confusion

Stained with heavy metal dye,
two sites explode into ambiguous
nebulae—the film of your breast
is filled with a shattering radiance,

a seeming cosmos shows millions
of light years bearing news
of the zooming origin and end
of life, but clouds of cysts

and fibroids hide what might be
an occult cancer, the malignancy
of those dark clusters can't be
ruled out. I take refuge from

imminent diagnosis by adding
columns of figures, reckoning last
year's expenses, preparing to meet
our accountant and pay our taxes.

Benghazi

Before this crisis, who'd ever heard
of Benghazi? And before Wednesday
four weeks ago, who'd have guessed
that your weakness climbing up stairs
was not the result of ten-hour days
with students at a Bed-Stuy high school
but breast cancer? Now every sign
of anxiety or low thyroid function
looks like a death sentence, as we sit
mesmerized by the news, waiting
for some benevolent power to
stop the despot's army in its drive
through the desert, it is already
within firing range of the city
whose fate chance has tied to yours.
We watch the carcasses of rebel cars
burning on the road to Benghazi
and in the central square, hapless
protesters mill around, prepared to die.

—3/19/2011

Inside the Imaging Machine

1

You've gone
in a striped
white and
black gown
down a
corridor
where I
can't follow
you—gone

inside the imaging
machine

shot up
with con-
trast fluid
forced to
lie still
an hour
enduring
a needle
biopsy

what fan-
tasies are
spinning
inside you
shut in that
long white
cylinder

"pass the
gun"
one of them
says and
it drills
into you
extracting
dyed tissue
from your
right breast

I glaze
over mes-
merized by
a seascape
on the wall
opposite me
in the waiting
room

2

Gazing
at the hooded
waves breaking
into lace of
spume I
fade into the
blur where
the sea drowns
under a gauzy
horizon

I lose
sight
of you
by be-
coming you

couvade
has its limits
leaves me
confined
among my
own images

I imagine
myself dying
near a window
waiting for
a white sail
to come into
view

sunk in a
stupor
on a shore
where your
cries can't
reach me

3

"Come back"
I tell myself
"to this waiting
room"

I'm delivered
out of one
reverie only
to slip
into another

I see you
pulling a black
scarf off your
head to show
me your bald
skull I face
your fury
and shame
at what awaits
you the black
emblem you're
flapping in
my direction
has me flying
toward you

in a death
ship where my
cries can't
reach you

Awakening

You're six years younger than I and take
pleasure in hiking up the side of a mountain.
At 67, I carry my body slowly
down the two flights of stairs in our home.

Crossing streets, if the curb is steep, you
reach for my hand and help me maintain my balance.
In your eyes, I see watchfulness grow
an outstretched arm, determined

to keep mortality from me, although
it's begun unraveling me at the joints
between grinding bones, on arthritic knees,
I walk around with two or three chronic conditions.

On these you concentrate your daily practice
of caring for me. And I keep my spine straight,
my mind alert, paying attention to my breath
as I exhale myself out to the cosmos.

So I wasn't particularly aware of fearing
my death, yet
my spiritual health was a fantasy.
I never thought you could die

before me, I imagined myself surrounded
by your devotion until my last
hour on earth. Now this: cancer,
proliferating microscopically for years,

has invaded your lymph nodes.
Will you lose your breast? Will I
lose you? Again I sink
into the dread that sickened me

when I first set out, running
into the ground-
lessness that began six feet
from my mother's arms, a vise

that bound me against her
so tightly, for safety's sake,
I couldn't breathe if I was
too close or too far from her.

Encounter with a Swordsman

I saw him at the bottom
of a sloping street. He
lumbered toward me
on the arm of his wife,
a semblance of the man
who'd had a powerful
impact on me. His gait
no longer gave any hint

of quickness. His skin
was pulled taut over the bones
of his face. His pants,
bunched into folds about
his waist, were cinched
by a belt that had become too
big for him, and hung
from its buckle, limp.

In heaps at the curb,
leaves stirred
and scratched against the ground
where they were driven. Clouds
that looked like continents
drifted
into the blue. He worked
his way toward where

I'd stopped for him.
A dry shudder
in the leaves, the wind
moving through them, and the clouds
pushed on, slowly

changing—a moment
in the life of the planet
was passing. I'd last seen him

on the day the buds broke
into blossom in Prospect Park.
He'd taken his stand
on top of Lookout Hill
amid a circle of elms among
whom he practiced
as though he were one
of them. And I, not to

intrude, stayed to a side,
waiting for him to flare
into existence as a
man cutting through the knot,
on which he trained his gaze,
with one all-out stroke
of his sword. For what seemed
hours, days, I waited

alongside him, with nothing
to relieve the tedium
of mere being, pain
shot through my motionless
body, my mind racing
in fantasy away
from the agitation I couldn't bear
to feel—the sun

glinted along the edge
of his sword and it was done
before I could see it

coming. He invited me to sit
zazen with him, I went
a few times, but
he just sat facing the wall in absolute
stillness, he was too severe

a companion for me. Now
he stood before me and asked,
"How are you?" I told him, "My wife
has stage two breast cancer."
He said, "A year
of torture." And in answer
to the question he read
in my eyes, his finger turned

into a knife, cutting
something out of his gut. "Colon
cancer. I'll be OK." This inter-
change happened in the early
weeks of your illness before we
knew what we were in for.
Immediately, I felt grateful
and leaned forward: to bow.

A year set a term on what
presently seemed an eternity.
A year, I thought. That
I can live with. He returned
my bow, and we went on
to talk about this and that,
and the clouds went on
in their own direction.

Housework

Blessed be dishes to wash, praise
the garbage that has to be gathered
and bagged and left at the curb.
Each morning I wake up frightened
and give thanks to the bed
where we've lain sleepless side-
by-side, for the crumpled sheets
and disordered blankets
ask nothing of me that I can't do,
so I get out of bed and make it
like the military rack with hospital
corners that a boy in boot camp,
gives his all to make perfect.

Through suffering, the old masters say,
comes knowledge. One day you were well;
the next, something boundless and terrifying
that looked like the Milky Way was found
in your breast. Whirled into this cosmos
where your death assumed its first
plausible shape, attempting to cope with
my grief and dread, I can't escape
seeing the mother I fled from as a boy
emerge in the housewifely response
that this affliction calls up in me.
Yet I'm not appalled to recognize
how much I'm like my mother in this crisis.

What's happened to my being oppressed
by the rage and disillusionment she held
at bay as she flew through her household
with a mop, making the floors under her slippers

shine? From her, I've inherited housework
as a substitute religion. One might think:
what a pitiful piece of self-knowledge
to have gained by facing the mortality
of my wife. Or I might receive
the unfamiliar feeling—gratitude
toward my mother—and raise the thanks
I've bestowed on inanimate objects to her
whom I now find has given me something good:

a default ritual, a resource that's helped
me hover above the abyss where my other
faculties failed. Ah, mother, gifted
girl-child of immigrants, consigned to the family
ghetto by centuries of anxiety your mother
exhaled in sighs that wove a circle
of overprotection around you, while the world
of strangers beckoned—how long
could you waste your life washing dishes
and dusting furniture and polishing floors?
How strange that the thing you wanted
to escape became your source of comfort!
On those endless afternoons in our over-

heated apartment, with its hissing
radiators, I invented magic arts to elude
you, mother, you never knew
that while you were wiping me
out through the silent treatment, I grew
invisible and walked through walls
to the cozy little hell where I thought you couldn't
reach me—you, pouring your will to mastery
into the housework that enslaved you,
transformed it into a rite of purification,

the discipline through which you exorcised dirt
from our home. That labor informed my soul
and became your gift to me of a means of survival.

Metastasis

In the privacy of our home,
the incision site goes on leaking

longer than expected, whitish
bits mixed in with blood

have you worried; our world
contracts to the areas

of your wounds and the appointed
times of caring for them

and meeting your doctors.
As we ride through the streets

of the Upper East Side,
it's hard to remember that

we are in the same city
where we marched against

one invasion after another
for forty-five years and

the site of 9/11 remains
a vast hole, a battle

ground where money
people and other power

brokers fight over
the shape of meaning

they want to impose on
our memory of the event.

In whichever segregated
unstable domain I imagine us

standing—in public or
private—we are

adrift among proliferating
ominous signs.

Black Site

On the day your surgeon says the incision
in your breast is healing beautifully, you tell me,
"Everything's going wrong." For you,
the suppurating wound in your arm pit
is everything: physical pain without letup
drains you of hope, you're carried away by its extraordinary
rendition to the place where nothing exists
but the absolute. There you are alone.
It would only add to your isolation if I
were to insist that logic and the law
of contradiction still applies to your case.
The bracelet around your wrist identifies you
as patient Santner, women in uniform
lead you through locked doors to the small rooms
where they put you out. When you wake up,
more of you is missing. One procedure follows
another. You know what drowning on dry land feels like
to a Muslim prisoner: real. Much as I yearn
for you to join me in the benign country
of common sense, it would be a betrayal of love
for me to try to refute the truth of despair.

The Eye of Your Pain

Pain's not monotonous to you: it shifts,
now gradually, now abruptly, as it ranges
up and down the scale of its intensity,
it switches back and forth among six
different modes—burning, itching, tightening
of the skin, tingling, numbness, shooting
pain—minor and major variations of the same
patterns make it forever
new

Pain seizes you by the lips of the small incision
under your right arm and squeezes you
there, subtle sadist, keeping you ever-vigilant,
relaxing its grip, and just as you start
to breathe quietly, it blindsides you, poking
you in the unhealed wound shaped like an eye
that hasn't stopped staring at me
since you cast out shame and lifted your arm
and showed me its
pit

I can't help
seeing something viscous at its center—
a moist blotch of dead
tissue, a dull gray smear that reflects light—
something that looks like the pupil of an eye
glazed over by glaucoma burns the pain
of your wound into my body, day and night
it doesn't stop crying blood flecked with
pus

Hour after hour you've favored your wounded
shoulder, now it's frozen in place, pain
erases the person you were in your life
as a beautiful woman, you feel like a stroke
victim, but refuse to be bound by this
condition, what contortions you go through
to unbutton your shirt and unstrap your surgical
corset and pull out the old pad and put in the
new

Look! you hold before me the stain that's come
out of you in less than an hour of drainage,
it's double the size of the wound, the wound
that's less than two centimeters in length—
no matter—it slices in half
your former intactness and widens into
the enormity of impingement through which pain
enters your body and takes possession of
you

In the Year of Chemotherapy

I've met the warrior in you
before, but never saw you fight
like this: you take to your bed
when some weird new symptom
racks you, as if to preempt
long uncertain hours of wasting
away and leap to the closure
of lying dead in your grave,
you sleep and dream and time
passes, you learn to decipher
the pain and contain your dread—

then hurl despair from you,
and you're back in your own after-
noon, in the hour of the blessed
ordinary, you pick up
flounder for dinner, bake it
between layers of tomato and onion,
season it with garlic and black
pepper, and call us to the table
which you set in the face
of death, in the midst of life.

In Sickness as in Health

Before bed, I move two chairs
from the dining room table and place
them face to face. I wash
my hands and sit down with you.
You unbutton your shirt and lift your bra
and I reach up and pinch
the tube at the point where it enters your skin.
The site where twenty lymph nodes
were removed and a catheter sewn into the wound
is too tender to be touched. I take great care
not to pull on the sutures, the slightest pressure
on the sensitive area brings pain.
I stop and start over again.
With the thumb and forefinger of my other hand,
the left one, I squeeze the clots and milk
the reddish-white fluid into the suction bulb,
which I empty into a measuring container.
I record the day's drainage and flush it down
the toilet. I've always been terribly queasy.
But I knew, as the nurse was showing me how
to care for your wound, that this procedure would be
transformed by my tenderness and your trust
into an act of utmost intimacy.

Outburst

Every day I wake up exhausted
and promise myself that I'll make
sabbath, I'll stop
bearing this lugubrious
body with its diffuse load
of yawns and sighs
to the desk where I dither,
hoping some metaphor will turn
up and recognize me and take me
out of my stifling routine.

How I long to break
out of the composure
that I have to keep up in caring
for a wife with cancer
and patients who bring me
amorphous hidden selves
tightly wrapped in obligations,
jump-started by ideals.

Yet the lyric work that promises
me a fresh start
turns into another task-
master that demands hard labor,
even the new song
that comes to my lips doesn't
let me slip
out of character, the one
to which I was harnessed
so long ago it seems natural
that I should assume
the identity that keeps me going:
a Jewish male, a mentsh, an old mule
tied to my daily round.

Oh, to lose myself in the sea
and sink to the bottom
and lie there, with the lung capacity of a whale,
then breach the waves with a great outburst
and just keep going, eating the wind
on wings that don't melt in the sun.

The Ordinary Life

Eight weeks ago you were
diagnosed with breast cancer.

I walked out into the day, surprised
by bees in our yard, despite

their bizarre and terrifying die-off
elsewhere, they returned

to the briefly-flowering dogwood
you planted 24 years ago

when we moved into our house.
Nothing special, but the very

ordinariness of it astonished me
as I watched them hover

above the blossoms and dive in
to collect nectar and cover

their bodies in pollen, life-
gladness returned, and poetry,

which had left me bereft
by its absence,

came like bees to your tree,
so that I might live

with catastrophe in the world
of signs and wonders.

Love's Body

My love's body
is
being racked
by an occult cancer.

In pain, she cares
about the impact
of her pain on me,

and the love we enjoyed
every day in good
health grows acute in illness.

•

Love, being married
to you teaches me more
about what I am
here for
than my liberal arts education
and erratic mindfulness practice.

My self-
preoccupation dissolves
in this crisis.
I am all tenderness
in your presence.

With my body
in the grip of what you're living
through—a throbbing
in the arm pit

where your lymph nodes were
removed, a reverb
in the chest of slicing
the hidden
tumors out of your breast—
we sit in silence,
celebrating the marriage
of flesh and air.

•

The sage physician
and rabbi, Maimonides, holds
that unfamiliar bodily sensations
are a sign
that an angel is speaking
to him in the language
of vibrations.

He translates his belief
into being attuned
and grasping
the full severity of compassion moving
through him in sound waves
that touch more subtle receptors
than human ears
and reach beyond the elisions
of physical speech.

•

Here in the room
with you, my attention
is pitched to pick up
things that can't be

said, and I receive the blessing
and wound
that Maimonides knew
as intercourse with an angel.

●

Here, I am given
the capacity to endure
not knowing
how things will work
out, despite the wish
for definite knowledge
that afflicts me
elsewhere, with you
I have the tenacity
not to lose
contact with the angel
sent by Maimonides
to tune my perplexed
self to one major key,
the C of faith.

Wisteria

I sit down at a small table
with your cancer
on my mind, besotted
by sadness.

Two days after your latest
surgery, and you're back
at work, your door open
to students who come
and go, bringing you trouble
they can talk over
with no other adult—work
you love more than ever.

And I sit facing the wall
with my fingers on the keys
of my Wheelwriter,
I go back to the room
where you're tortured
by the treatment that keeps you
alive, stuck with needles,
tied to a chemo chair, I
join you there, give you ice
to suck on, stroke
your hair, but the comfort I want
to bring you doesn't suffice
to stop the pain.

The scene changes: now
I'm with you at a wrought
iron table in our garden.

The fence is transformed by
a vine into a veil of white
blossoms: wisteria
is gradually tearing it down
while holding open
house for bees.

Its branches writhe
through slats,
tearing them apart and flowering
on both sides of the fence.

You catch my eyes narrowing
on the damage, and take my hand
in yours. A storm passes
between your body and mine,
a shudder that marries destruction
and awakening to more life.

IV. After a Brief Visit to Herring Point

> Let there be an expanse in the midst of the water,
> that it may separate water from water.
> —Genesis 1:6

On This Shore
to Paul Gorrin

I walked with my friend
to the edge of the continent.

We stood side by side for a while
facing the ocean

and the sky
melded with it that night into one dark

limitlessly friendly expanse
that went on beyond anything we could see,

we heard the continuo
of the waves, the wind

brushed our cheeks, the history
of our having traveled together

over the course of a lifetime
dropped away and

we were in the midst
of a moment that exceeded what we sought

to name and celebrate
by coming here. As if

we were just one
person, we turned at the same time

and went back into
the light of the known

worlds we live in. Now I am
in Brooklyn, and he is in a small

town in Delaware, but
the room where I sit

and his room open
onto the same sea.

At Herring Point

1

After returning home, I try to
find where I've been. Herring Point
is too small and unfrequented to appear
in *The Mapquest Standard Road Atlas.*

Around the spot where I stood, dots
mark the place where memory
reaches beyond our lifetime:
these are towns and villages

with names like Hardscrabble,
Workmans Corner, Bryans Store,
Hitchens, Crossroads, Pepperbox,
Old Furnace, I must have driven

through some of them in the dark.
Men grown silent with lack
of work, with disability,
with humiliation, women stoic

with disappointment in marriage,
with unsobbed grief—
such were the people with
whom I celebrated the new

office opened by their doc,
my old friend Paul. Now I read
that their forebears gave
the names of their lives to

their place in the world,
lest they pass out of it
without leaving a trace
on the map of America.

2

Paul and I drive off after
the ribbon-cutting ceremony
to a spit of land between Delaware
Bay and the Atlantic
that he wants to show me.

We leave our car on the side
of the road, proceed on foot
through a gate
with a sign that says no one
may go beyond this point

without a fishing license.
We go on anyway,
holding the winding path
by slivers of moonlight
that pick it out of a maze

of dunes and reeds,
and a compass of sound
keeps us oriented—
the thrashing of waves
just ahead repeats

two phrases: keep going,
it's just ahead. I didn't know
until I relived it in memory
that I was translating sensations
into little mantras

that guided me on. I'd come
all the way from New York
to stand with Paul
on this day, a milestone
in his life. And I let go

of the anxiety that gripped
me when we started
walking around in the dark.
The brights of two trucks
flood the night, die

down abruptly, and we see
no more of them, the men
who come here to fish for tomorrow
night's dinner. In the darkness
that flares and blinds me

after they pass, I feel
my whole body frantically dilate, afraid
we will not reach the ocean.
And the next moment, the moon
is riding the waves, toward us.

Make Your Home Here

Between the ocean and the bay
I'm told ions attach themselves
to allergens and they fall
out of the air we breathe.

Given my ignorance
of the scientific laws that rule
this world, I believe
it's true and confirms my experience

that a beneficent process
incarnating itself as a god
made this place sacred
to its healing operation.

I found this out years ago
when I came into an immense
wakefulness every time
I walked along the beach

between Jamaica Bay and the whole
Atlantic. I can testify
that in this area as no other
I become free

of irritation in the lungs
and heaviness of the brains
I bear elsewhere.
If I had any sense

I would listen
to this place where I am
not pulled down in chronic
illness. On the strand

between two bodies of water
a new life would be possible
for me. Breathing here
brings home the truth of it.

But already I hear Habit,
the great deadener,
stopping my ears
against the sea's whisperings.

Vows

Austerity always appealed to me more
than greed. And each day I renewed
my vows against it. There are opposing

ways to tell any story. You might ask:
Then how come each night at 3 a.m.
when the hour of hunger struck

my legs carried my belly on arthritic
knees down two flights of pain
and I stood before the open

refrigerator, ransacking its innards
with my eyes while my mouth gorged?
Or you could say: In spite

of an endless stream of defeat
I began each day with the hope
that on this night I'd be different.

It's Not Too Late—If

It's not too late—if
I were to take seriously
where my happiness lies
I would stop

being this old mule
who has more important things
to do than waste
a week-end traveling

to see my friend of more
than forty-five years
and drive into a forest
along the Atlantic coast

and get out of the car
and follow the sandy trail
without a flashlight, guided
by the heave and crash

of the breakers ahead
and stand with our backs
to terra firma on the receding
shore, just listening

Before the Firmament

There, the curve of the earth was no more.
Everything poured into everything, sky
into water, water and sky joined in one
limitless time of potential space before

God is said to have separated them
with a *raki'a*, an expanse, the word
for hammering metal or flattening
earth. A few stars were enough

to keep the illusion that I was
in the midst of a chaos saturated
with peace from enduring beyond
the experience of no horizon.

This was the instant before
artisanal eyes seized the lights
of the heavens and wrested out of them
such signs as we place everywhere

in the cosmos, so we may find our way back
to these waterless waters and be
wholly immersed again in formlessness
without fear of drowning.

Snow Geese

A child of Yiddish
actors, you come to the Broadkiln
to hunt snow geese.
You stand with your shotgun
ready, hidden
in a blind and yes
you fire and yes
you bring down a few birds.

Foreign as this is to me
I can imagine how for you
this feels like Americanization
like winning
a place for yourself at the hunter's table
the only Jew among
your neighbors in a town
where everyone has a gun in the house
and all social divisions melt
over the male meals at the hunt club.

I note with pleasure what stayed
with you as your own
discovery from the first time
you stood from sunup to sundown
in a blind: at dawn
when the geese are flying to the east
the plumage of their breast
is a glistening, a hammered gold—
your words as you reminisced—
and when they return in the evening
to their resting place, the red shift
of sunlight entering our atmosphere
is visible as the deeper gold
on their breast feathers, free of blue.

For days after noticing this, you
pored over your old physics texts
to work out what forces have to converge
for this slight transfiguration
of the mundane to reward you
for standing still and keeping watch
over one whole day.

The Return

1

I awoke today in the middle
of a dream, a forest
of towering spruce screened me
from the shoulder where
we'd pulled off the road
and parked a month ago
outside the gate to Herring Point.

I'd walked into the dark
woods so that no one
could see or hear
me pissing, yet the grasses
shivering on all sides of me
took shape as an Iroquois
hunter running unseen
through the centuries within
ear-shot, I was
at the mercy of a master
of surprise and speed and invisible
survival in this place
where I was ill-equipped
to live, a child again, trembling
as he encircled me
to protect his land from
my casual desecration of it.

By the time I'd zipped up
my fly and rushed back
to the road, I had no memory
of my encounter with him.

But early this morning, he
came back to me in a dream
as the spirit of the place,
who opened me
to the wonder and terror
of Herring Point, and I lived
through my night there
again from the beginning.

2

Details that were blurred when we moved
through them came into focus, black letters
there to arrest us leapt from the yellow
sign: No Trespassing—No One
Without A Fishing License May Enter Here.

Without a word, we unlatched the gate
and set out, making our way
through a maze of dunes toward
the ocean, the undertone
that rattled each of us separately
stopped. In its abrupt cessation,
we could sense what we had come through—
the dread of openness we live with

was gone. There was only this
tide, this night, this
bright moon, these sandpipers
writing nervous indecipherable runes
along this shore where we stood
side-by-side, listening.

3

On this narrow strand
set apart as a sanctuary
for wildlife between Delaware
Bay and the gray Atlantic,
we heard water dispersed
in clouds by last week's heat
wave, and restored to the sea
in yesterday's downpour,
heaving and soughing
as it returned to land.
Nothing obstructed the horizon
over which no face
hovered. Yet we lacked
nothing. Cool air
from limitless expanses
brushed our cheeks
and went through us,
releasing fear, fear
that we carried in the stone
jar of the lungs, in the knot
of the stomach, we ceased
holding onto the hunger that eats
our capacity for being
alive to the world:
we stood on a hairsbreadth
between the sea inside us
and the one without
and there was neither
the one nor the two of us.

4

And now I wonder, dear
friend, what of all this
can I retain? Am I falling
into my usual error—
clinging to the good
experience? Is the urge
to be exalted the birth-
right of the soul or a source
of confusion, or something
of both? Questions that lead
away from the living
moment. I stood
at a place emptied
of hindrances to being
at peace, listening
to the waves, incessant variations
of whooshing and withdrawing under the night
sky. Isn't it time
I took up residence
on the site of loss,
in the house of my wavering,
my impurity and impermanence?

How far I am
from that in my own home,
trying to shut out small
disturbances, my attention broken
by Jehovah's Witnesses ringing my bell,
cold calls from stock brokers,
and the old woman with dyed
orange-blond hair, my neighbor,
starving for a friendly word

from passersby, sits
for hours on a beach
chair with her little yapping
lapdog under my window.

How can I remain calm
in the midst of such
noise? It's a dream
to think that I can remain anywhere
at all. Isn't it
time that I gave up
striving to keep out
the dark I always return to?
Time
that I took up trespassing
into the world I encountered at Herring Point.

The Waves

At the edge of land,
you stand still, watching the ocean heave
and contract: you see

the density and transparency
of the same wave,

it rears six feet
into the air, letting light through
as it crests and crashes,

it bears you into
the immensity of disappearing
from yourself for a while.

•

At high tide, it's possible
to take the sea
as a kind of scripture:

it explodes and washes away
the language of terra firma
that you live by.

Here creation speaks in tongues
of water that you remember
from before you were born,

the waves roar
and soothe
and exceed the concepts

that funnel goods
of the solid world into red
and black columns of self-

interest. Suddenly
you cease
striving to force life

to fit your wish
for seas without volcanoes
below

that go off without reference
to your notion of gain
and loss.

Acknowledgments

Thanks to the editors of the magazines in which these poems appeared:

The Manhattan Review: "Janus," "The Burning Hoop," "Stranded Objects," "Metastasis," "Before the Firmament," "Snow Geese"

Hanging Loose: "Days of Kivi," "Shiva for Kivi," "In Sickness as in Health"

Kerem: "Displaced Persons"

Hamilton Stone Review: "The Knot"

The Saint Ann's Review: "In the Year of Chemotherapy," "Make Your Home Here," "It's Not Too Late—If," "Vows"

Thanks to Allan Appel, Allen Bergson, Philip Fried, Pam Laskin, Ellen Maddow, Deena Metzger, Dennis Nurkse, Maddy Santner, Mark Solomon, Mark Weiss, Sue Willis, Eileen Wiseman, and Paul Zimet.

A Note about the Author

MARC KAMINSKY is a poet, essayist, and psychotherapist in private practice in Brooklyn. He is the author of eight previous books of poetry, including *The Road from Hiroshima* (Simon and Schuster), *Daily Bread* (University of Illinois Press) and *Kafka's Ax* (forthcoming from Junction Press in 2018). His poems have appeared in many magazines and anthologies, including *Voices within the Ark: The Modern Jewish Poets, Atomic Ghost*, and *The Oxford Book of Aging*. He has published six books and many essays on aging, reminiscing and storytelling, and the culture of Yiddishkeit.

Author photo by Madelaine Santner.

For the full Dos Madres Press catalog:
www.dosmadres.com

Printed by Libri Plureos GmbH in Hamburg, Germany